Original title:
The Snowbound Night

Copyright © 2024 Swan Charm
All rights reserved.

Author: Olivia Oja
ISBN HARDBACK: 978-9916-79-603-0
ISBN PAPERBACK: 978-9916-79-604-7
ISBN EBOOK: 978-9916-79-605-4

Shimmering Twilight

The sun dips low, a golden hue,
Whispers of dusk in colors new.
Clouds catch fire, a fleeting blaze,
Nature's canvas, a breathtaking gaze.

Stars awaken, the nightbirds sway,
Softly calling for the end of day.
Shadows stretch, a gentle sigh,
As twilight glimmers, the world slips by.

Embers in the Chill

The fire crackles, warmth divine,
Embers dancing, soft and fine.
Winter's breath, a frosty chill,
Yet inside glows a fervent thrill.

Blankets wrapped 'round every frame,
Hearts ignite with whispered names.
Outside, the world is crisp and stark,
But within, we light our spark.

Nightfall's Embrace

As daylight fades, the stars appear,
Nightfall whispers, drawing near.
Silhouettes of trees in flight,
Under the blanket of the night.

A gentle hush, the world slows down,
Moonlight casts a silver crown.
Dreams take flight on velvet wings,
In night's embrace, the heart still sings.

Crystalline Dreams

In the quiet, crystals gleam,
Reflections weave a waking dream.
Frosty patterns, magic spun,
Whispers of winter's softest fun.

Through the window, glimmers bright,
A tapestry of purest light.
Each twinkle tells a secret tale,
Of snowy lands where hopes set sail.

Starlit Serenity on White Horizons

In the hush of night,
Stars sprinkle the sky,
Whispers of the wind,
Softly passing by.

A blanket of snow,
Covers earth's embrace,
Glistening like diamonds,
In the moon's gentle grace.

Trees stand still and proud,
Their branches lightly dressed,
Nature's quiet song,
A lullaby to rest.

Footprints mark the path,
Of wanderers so bold,
Stories left behind,
In the silence untold.

The world feels alive,
In this frozen sight,
A dance of pure peace,
In the stillness of light.

Ghosts of Dreams in Shimmering Snow

Upon the white drifts,
Memories take flight,
Specters of our dreams,
In the soft moonlight.

Each flake tells a tale,
Of wishes once spun,
Lost in the night air,
Under the pale sun.

Whispers of the past,
Echo in the breeze,
Inviting us to roam,
Among ancient trees.

Shadows flicker near,
In the evening's glow,
Hiding long-lost hopes,
In the shimmering snow.

Eyes closed in wonder,
We search for what's true,
The ghosts of our dreams,
Always guiding through.

Wanderers Beneath the Winter's Breath

Beneath the soft clouds,
Wanderers tread light,
In the frosty air,
With hearts bold and bright.

The chill wraps around,
A cloak of pure peace,
Breath visible like dreams,
In the cold's sweet release.

They journey through night,
Chasing stars up high,
With hopes like fireflies,
Twinkling in the sky.

Every step a story,
Written on the frost,
In the echoing silence,
Of what they have lost.

Beneath the vast sky,
In a world so still,
They carry the warmth,
Of longing and will.

Memories Frozen in Moonlight

Moonlight bathes the world,
In a silvery hue,
Secrets frozen in stillness,
Waiting to break through.

Each shadow a whisper,
Of days long gone by,
Captured in the glow,
Of the night's gentle sigh.

Time stands on the brink,
Lost moments afloat,
In the stillness of night,
Like a fading note.

Hearts dance in the gleam,
Of an ethereal light,
As memories resurface,
In the depth of night.

Frozen yet alive,
In the luminous stream,
We visit the past,
In the shapeless dream.

The Sound of Stillness in a Snowy Realm

In the quiet glow of dusk,
Snowflakes dance on chilly breeze.
Whispers weave through frosted trees,
Nature holds her breath in hush.

Footsteps fade into the night,
Buried deep under white shrouds.
Silence wraps the world so tight,
Every echo lost in clouds.

Stars emerge with gentle grace,
Painting dreams on velvet sky.
In the stillness, hearts embrace,
As time drifts softly by.

Winter's Lullaby at the Blanket's Edge

Snowy blankets cradle sleep,
Cotton clouds, a serene sight.
Crickets hum their lullaby,
Underneath the silver light.

Fires crackle with soft glow,
Casting shadows, warm and deep.
Windchimes play a tune, though low,
As the world begins to weep.

Dreams take flight on frosty wings,
Floating high, through bracing night.
Winter sings of tender things,
Holding love, in softest light.

Echoing Footsteps in a White Wonderland

Footsteps crunch on powdered ground,
Echoes call from far away.
In this realm, it's peace I've found,
Where shadows of the night play.

Trees stand tall in cloaks of white,
Guarding secrets of the land.
Stars glance down with twinkling light,
As night's tapestry is planned.

Whispers of the winter's breath,
Chill the air with gentle sighs.
In the silence there's no death,
Just the dance of snowflakes' lies.

A Night of Pearls Beneath Frosty Skies

Underneath the frosty skies,
Pearls of light begin to gleam.
Each a wish from whispered sighs,
In the heart, they softly teem.

Moonlight drapes a silver cloak,
Over fields so still and bright.
Every breath, a tender stroke,
Painting whispers in the night.

Beneath stars like brightened seas,
Nights like these, we find our way.
Nature hums, a soothing breeze,
Guiding dreams until the day.

A Symphony of Frost and Starlight

Whispers of winter in the night,
Crystals dance beneath the moonlight.
Each breath a cloud, soft and white,
Wrapped in silence, pure delight.

Stars twinkle like distant dreams,
While snowflakes weave their silver seams.
Nature hums, or so it seems,
In this symphony of frozen beams.

The trees stand tall, dressed in white,
Guardians of the shimmering sight.
Embracing the chill, the hearts ignite,
Held captive by the beauty's light.

Beneath the sky, a canvas vast,
Footprints echo, memories cast.
The cold wraps tightly, shadows cast,
In the stillness, our thoughts amassed.

In the glow of dawn, hope will rise,
Frosted wishes, painted skies.
With every breath, the heart complies,
In this world of wonder, we are wise.

The Unseen Paths of Frosted Wishes

Amidst the whispers of the breeze,
Frosted wishes dance with ease.
Nature's magic, intertwined,
In shadows deep, our hearts aligned.

Footprints lead to hidden dreams,
Where moonlight glows and starlight beams.
Every pathway wrapped in white,
Guiding souls through the night.

The world asleep in blankets cold,
Tales of wonder yet untold.
Each flake a wish, a gentle thought,
In this stillness, we are caught.

Over valleys, silence reigns,
Echoes linger, sweet refrains.
Every moment, perfect bliss,
In the frosted air, we reminisce.

As dawn approaches, colors bloom,
Frost will melt, dispel the gloom.
Yet in our hearts, the wishes stay,
Guiding us on our chosen way.

Wingbeats in the Stillness of Night

In the quiet, softly heard,
Flutters of wings, a gentle bird.
Silhouettes dance in shadows light,
Whispers echo in the night.

Moonlight kisses the velvet sky,
As creatures soar and spirits fly.
Each heartbeat syncs with the breeze,
Nature stirs with graceful ease.

Dreams take flight on silver wings,
In the stillness, freedom sings.
Chasing stars 'neath the infinite,
In this moment, we are lit.

Through branches woven, paths unknown,
The night unfolds, a world of its own.
Every rustle tells a tale,
Of adventures where spirits sail.

As dawn creeps in, soft and warm,
Birds retreat, away from harm.
Yet in our hearts, the whispers stay,
Woven in twilight's gentle sway.

Ebony Trees Under Silver Skies

Rooted deep in silent grace,
Whispers float in twilight's face.
Branches stretch like ancient dreams,
Dancing softly with moonbeams.

Shadowed forms in calm repose,
Nature's calm, the stillness grows.
Leaves murmur tales of yesteryear,
Underneath, the world feels near.

Stars are scattered, diamonds bright,
Woven into the fabric of night.
Ebony silhouettes arise,
A chorus swells beneath the skies.

Each gust carries a secret quest,
In the dark, the heart finds rest.
Wisdom whispers from above,
In the night, we find the love.

Glimmers dance in velvet air,
Among the trees, dreams layer.
Silver skies, with stories vast,
In their brilliance, shadows cast.

Frosted Cloak

Winter drapes a frosted cloak,
Silence falls, no echoes spoke.
Snowflakes kiss the earth below,
In their dance, a gentle glow.

Crystals spark in morning light,
Transforming day from dark to bright.
Whispers of the chill surround,
Nature's breath, a subtle sound.

Trees adorned in glistening white,
Stand tall against the fading night.
Every branch, a jeweled crown,
In this wonderland, we drown.

Children laugh in playful glee,
Building dreams, so wild and free.
Footsteps crunch in rhythmic cheer,
A fleeting moment, held so dear.

As sunset paints the sky anew,
The world glows in every hue.
Wrapped in warmth, we find our place,
In winter's tender, soft embrace.

Hibernal Hymn

In the stillness of the night,
Creatures rest, bowing to the light.
Underneath the snowy shroud,
Nature sings, both soft and loud.

Golden dreams in slumber deep,
Secrets of the earth to keep.
Gentle sighs of whispered frost,
In this quiet, nothing's lost.

Branches bare, their stories told,
In the chill, we find the bold.
Life slows down, as shadows creep,
While the world falls fast asleep.

Moonlight casts a silver glow,
Guiding all who wish to know.
In the hibernal peace we find,
A melody that stirs the mind.

With each dawning's early light,
Hope awakens from the night.
Softly then, a hymn will rise,
Echoing beneath vast skies.

Luminous Nightfall

As dusk drapes the world in dreams,
Colors blend, the horizon gleams.
Whispers float on evening air,
Crafting magic everywhere.

Stars emerge, a painted sea,
Infinite, wild, bold, and free.
Luminous dots across the sky,
Glimmers of hopes that will not die.

In the dark, the shadows play,
Fleeting phantoms on their way.
Moonlight weaves a silver thread,
Guiding souls to places spread.

Nightfall brings a gentle pause,
A moment's breath, without a cause.
Softly, dreams begin to stir,
While the night starts to confer.

Each heartbeat blends with twilight's song,
In this realm, we all belong.
Luminous nightfall draws us close,
In its embrace, we find repose.

A Blanket of Softness

In the quiet of dawn's embrace,
A tender touch, a warm space.
Gentle whispers, soft and light,
Wrapped in dreams, the world feels right.

Pastel hues in the morning glow,
A hush descends, a tranquil flow.
Nature breathes in calming sighs,
Underneath the vast, blue skies.

Fleecy clouds drift overhead,
Cradling hopes that softly spread.
Each tender moment, pure and sweet,
In this haven, hearts can meet.

A blanket spreads across the earth,
Embracing us in gentle mirth.
With every heartbeat, love ignites,
In this warmth, all pain unites.

As the day wanes to a close,
The softness lingers, gently flows.
Under starlight, dreams take flight,
In a blanket of softness, lies the night.

Shards of Ice

Glistening crystals scatter light,
A frozen world, both sharp and bright.
Silent echoes in the pale air,
Beauty wrapped in fragile care.

Each shard reflects a tale untold,
Of winter's grasp, a fierce hold.
Nature's sculptor at work divine,
Etching artistry, cold and fine.

The biting wind sings a chill song,
Where fleeting moments feel so wrong.
Yet within this stark, crisp embrace,
Lies a wonder, a hidden grace.

A glance reveals a fleeting fire,
In heartbeats cold, igniting desire.
A paradox in frigid air,
Shards of ice, a love laid bare.

As the sun melts the frozen seam,
The shards dissolve, a waking dream.
Yet the memory, sharp and nice,
Will linger long, these shards of ice.

Where Shadows Rest

Beneath the boughs where shadows lay,
A quiet refuge, far away.
The sunlight dances through the leaves,
In this haven, the heart believes.

Whispers echo in the dusk,
A soft embrace, a familiar musk.
Petals fall like silent tears,
Capturing whispers of the years.

In twilight's arms, the world feels slow,
Tranquil moments begin to flow.
Each heartbeat found in whispered themes,
As shadows weave through silver dreams.

Resting softly in the night,
The shadows blanket all in sight.
Here, secrets shared beneath the stars,
In this peace, we heal our scars.

Where shadows meet and silence speaks,
The world transforms; the soul seeks.
Among the stillness, love invests,
In the gentle place where shadows rest.

Whispers of Winter's Veil

Underneath a canopy so white,
Winter whispers, soft and light.
Each flake dances, a fleeting sight,
Nature's breath, pure and bright.

Frozen branches, shimmering lace,
A tranquil hush in every space.
Silence blankets the earth's embrace,
As time slows down its rapid pace.

In the stillness, a secret unfolds,
A warmth hidden in the cold holds.
Embers flicker, hearts align,
In winter's veil, love starts to shine.

Gentle winds through the pines sway,
Carrying dreams that softly play.
Whispers of hope, both calm and frail,
Echo through winter's delicate veil.

As twilight beckons, stars appear,
Winter's charm draws all so near.
In the quiet, with hearts unveiled,
We find our peace, 'neath winter's veil.

Frozen Echoes Beneath the Stars

In the stillness of the night,
Whispers dance on frozen air,
Stars above like distant lights,
Echoes linger everywhere.

Silent shadows softly creep,
Across the glimmering white,
Secrets that the cold winds keep,
Bathe the world in soft twilight.

Footprints trace a fleeting tale,
Of dreams wrapped in winter's fold,
As the icy winds prevail,
Through the silence, brave and bold.

Frozen echoes gently call,
Nature's breath in crystal hue,
In the quiet, hearts enthrall,
Beneath a vast, enchanting view.

Moments paused in winter's grace,
Time holds its breath, still as snow,
In this hushed, celestial space,
Frozen echoes come and go.

Moonlight on a Frosted Tapestry

Moonlight weaves a silken glow,
Across the fields of silent white,
Patterns form, as breezes blow,
Painting dreams in the night.

Frosted branches, sparkling bright,
Catch the shimmer, soft and clear,
Owls call out into the night,
While the stars begin to cheer.

Each flake glistens, pure and light,
Crafting beauty in the chill,
A tapestry of sheer delight,
Wrapped in winter's tranquil thrill.

Gentle shadows stretch and play,
Guided by the moon's embrace,
In this quiet, soft ballet,
Time slows down with steady grace.

Whispers drift on frosted air,
Every heartbeat sings of peace,
In the magic, we are bare,
As the night begins to cease.

Hushed Dreams in a Crystal World

In a world of frost and fire,
Dreams take flight on icy breeze,
Every moment, pure desire,
Hushed in whispers through the trees.

Snowflakes twirl like dancers fair,
Filling paths with magic bright,
Each a wish, a breath of air,
Sparking hope in winter's night.

Frosted petals glisten, gleam,
In the quiet, beauty flows,
Crystals weave a waking dream,
Where the heart's own warmth bestows.

Silence reigns, a gentle hush,
Blankets all in white embrace,
In this soft and snowy rush,
Time is lost, a stilling grace.

Hushed dreams settle, softly rest,
In the cradle of the cold,
Wrapped in nature's endless quest,
Stories waiting to unfold.

Enchanted Silence of the Snowfall

Whispers float on snowy trails,
As the world dons white attire,
In the air, enchantment sails,
Bringing hearts a warm desire.

Gentle flakes like feathered lace,
Wrap the ground in pure embrace,
Every moment holds a trace,
Of soft truths in nature's grace.

Silent nights where shadows blend,
Cloaked in whispers, soft and low,
Mysteries begin to mend,
As the beauty starts to flow.

Hushed beneath the winter's chill,
The stillness wraps the world anew,
Every heartbeat echoes will,
In a dance concealed from view.

Enchanted silence, we adore,
In the snowfall's gentle hold,
Winter's calm forevermore,
Stories told, and dreams retold.

Frozen Moments In Still Time

Time stands still in icy breath,
Whispers locked in frozen depth.
Footprints linger, soft and light,
Ghosts of warmth in winter's night.

Sunlight fades, a golden hue,
Kisses frost on limbs anew.
Silence dances, snowflakes fall,
A moment frozen, capturing all.

Branches glimmer, branches sway,
Nature's beauty on display.
Heartbeats echo in the chill,
A lullaby of winter's will.

In the twilight, shadows creep,
Memories in silence seep.
Each glimmered flake, a tale untold,
Stories woven in strands of cold.

Embrace the stillness, feel the air,
Find the magic linger there.
Frozen moments, hold them tight,
A fleeting dream in winter's light.

Ethereal Glow of Winter's Heart

In the hush of twilight's grace,
A soft glow lights up the space.
Crisp and clear, the world aglow,
Winter's heart in gentle flow.

Stars awaken, twinkling bright,
Guiding lost souls in the night.
Whispers dance on frosty air,
In the stillness, dreams laid bare.

Moonlit pathways, silver sheen,
Nature wraps the world in dreams.
Each breath misty, each heartbeat slow,
In this magic, let love grow.

Snowflakes shimmer, tender kiss,
Wrapped in winter's whispered bliss.
Emotions bloom like flowers bright,
In the glow of snowy light.

Embrace the chill, the quiet grace,
Find your peace in winter's face.
Ethereal whispers, secrets shared,
In the heart of winter, loved and cared.

Frosted Secrets Beneath the Northern Sky

Beneath the vast and starry dome,
Frosted secrets call us home.
Underneath the quiet veil,
Our stories trapped in icy scale.

Winds that travel, tales untold,
In the frost, a magic bold.
Each breath carries whispers sweet,
Echoes of hearts that daring meet.

Stars ripple in the frozen night,
Glimmering softly, pure delight.
Layered voices weave and sway,
In the frost, they find their way.

Frozen rivers, dreams afloat,
In the silence, we take note.
Nature's canvas, stark and bright,
Colored by the northern light.

Beneath this sky of icy dreams,
Life flows softly in moonbeams.
Frosted secrets, come and see,
In winter's heart, we're all set free.

Nocturnal Embrace of Snowy Fields

In the night, the fields lie still,
Snowflakes dance with gentle thrill.
A blanket white, soft and deep,
In this embrace, the world asleep.

Moonlight waltzes on the ground,
In the silence, peace is found.
Whispers wander with the breeze,
Through the trees, with grace they tease.

Shadows wane and soft lights glow,
Nature's magic, pure and slow.
Every flake, a secret kept,
In the stillness, dreams are wept.

Branches cradle piles of white,
Nocturnal whispers take their flight.
Stars look down with watchful eyes,
In snowy fields, where beauty lies.

Embrace the quiet, lose the race,
In this world, find your place.
Through snowy fields, hearts will soar,
In the night's embrace, forevermore.

Frosted Breath and Quiet Thought

In the stillness of the night,
Where whispers linger soft and bright,
Frosted breath escapes my lips,
Quiet thoughts in gentle slips.

Moonlight dances on the ground,
A silver glow, a sacred sound,
Footsteps echo, crisp and clear,
In this moment, all is dear.

Snowflakes twirl like fleeting dreams,
Caught in the moon's ethereal beams,
Nature's canvas, pure and white,
Frosted breath, a warm delight.

In solitude, my mind takes flight,
Through tranquil paths of starlit night,
Each breath woven with the cold,
Quiet stories yet untold.

Underneath the endless sky,
Thoughts like snowflakes drift and fly,
In the silence, I find my way,
Frosted breath and quiet sway.

Nightfall's Touch on a Shimmering Landscape

Nightfall weaves its velvet thread,
Over hills where shadows spread,
A shimmering landscape comes alive,
As darkness whispers, dreams arrive.

Stars emerge like diamonds rare,
Scattering light with tender care,
Each twinkle speaks a secret tale,
Of distant worlds beyond the veil.

Moonbeams kiss the grassy knolls,
While crickets sing to wandering souls,
The air is thick with mysteries,
Held softly in the evening breeze.

Reflections dance on silver streams,
Where nature cradles all our dreams,
In the hush, the night unfurls,
A tapestry of darkened pearls.

As shadows blend and night takes hold,
The shimmering landscape whispers bold,
With nightfall's touch, the magic grows,
In every corner, beauty flows.

Secrets Cradled in Snowy Silence

In the hush of snow's embrace,
Whispers linger, soft in grace,
Secrets cradle in the night,
Beneath a blanket pure and white.

Footprints mark the paths we've trod,
Echoes dance where once we plod,
Snowflakes fall like whispered sighs,
Carrying secrets to the skies.

A quiet world, where time stands still,
Woven dreams by winter's will,
In the silence, hearts entwine,
Cradled truths in snow, divine.

Each flake a story, unique and rare,
Softly shaping the frosty air,
In gentle silence, we confess,
Secrets wrapped in snow's caress.

Amidst the chill, we find our place,
In the wonder of winter's grace,
As snowy silence holds us tight,
With secrets woven into night.

Beneath the Icy Canopy

Beneath the icy canopy,
Where silence reigns, so wild and free,
Frosted branches arch above,
A world transformed by winter's love.

Shimmering crystals catch the light,
Creating beauty, pure and bright,
Each shimmer tells a fleeting tale,
Of seasons past and winter's veil.

The air is crisp, a gentle chill,
Nature breathes, with grace and to thrill,
In the shadows, magic stirs,
A silent song that softly purrs.

Underneath the tranquil sky,
Whispers of the past drift by,
In the embrace of cold's sweet breath,
Life pauses, defying death.

Beneath the branches, dreams take root,
In icy stillness, hope bears fruit,
Wrapped in winter's tender hand,
We find our peace in this quiet land.

Midnight Revelations Beneath White Stillness

In the hush of night, secrets rise,
Moonlight whispers, soft and wise.
Snowflakes drift through the air,
Nature's blanket, a tranquil stare.

Silent thoughts glide on the breeze,
Carried softly among the trees.
Stars loom bright, a shimmering guide,
Within their glow, hidden truths abide.

Footsteps echo on the snow,
Each print a tale of long ago.
Beneath the stillness, dreams unfold,
Wrapped in warmth as night turns cold.

Time surrenders to the calm,
Hearts embrace the night's sweet balm.
In the silence, worlds collide,
Mysteries deep within reside.

Awake to wonders, breathless, still,
Chasing shadows of the will.
Midnight's canvas, vast and bright,
Cradling souls in endless night.

Soft Footfalls on a Silken Sheet

Whispers glide on gentle air,
Barefoot dreams beyond compare.
Moonlit sheets in silver light,
Embrace the peace of quiet night.

Each step, a dance, a soft caress,
Through the dark, we acquiesce.
Embers fade, but warmth remains,
In this haven, love sustains.

Fingers trace the softest lines,
In this moment, heart entwines.
Silken threads of shared release,
Here we find our sweetest peace.

Time stands still on this warm bed,
Each thought like whispers left unsaid.
Breath to breath, our silence sings,
Wrapped in love, the night still clings.

Soft footfalls in the moon's embrace,
Chasing shadows, finding grace.
Within this space, our laughter glows,
Memory blooms, the heart's repose.

Shadows Dance on Frozen Breath

In the frost, shadows sway,
Echoes of the close of day.
Figures flicker on crisp air,
Dancing freely, without care.

Night unveils its dark delight,
Stars above weave threads of light.
Whispers cling to winter's chill,
As the heart bends to its will.

Frozen breath hangs in the cold,
Stories linger, yet untold.
In the dark, we lose our way,
Turned by tales the night will say.

Laughter echoes, bittersweet,
Frosted laughter, warm retreat.
Shadows play on winter's stage,
Life unfolds, page by page.

With each movement, spirits weave,
In the stillness, we believe.
Frozen breath and shadows cast,
In the moment, hearts hold fast.

Twinkling Lights in a Chilled Embrace

Stars above in velvet skies,
Twinkling softly, ancient sighs.
Wrapped in cold, a gentle glow,
Nighttime whispers, soft and slow.

Frosty air, a dance of warmth,
Beneath the lights, we find our charm.
Softly glowing, dreams unfold,
In this night, hearts brave and bold.

Hands entwined, we walk the path,
Chilled embrace, a love that lasts.
Lights like jewels upon the dark,
Every glance ignites a spark.

Every twinkle tells a tale,
Of the heart that will not stale.
In this moment, time stands still,
Under stars, we find our thrill.

Chilled embrace, but spirits rise,
Wrapped in warmth beneath the skies.
Twinkling lights in winter's breath,
Whisper love that conquers death.

A Canvas of White Under Midnight Stars

In the hush of night, all is still,
Snow coats the earth, a peaceful thrill.
Stars twinkle bright in the velvet dome,
A canvas of white where shadows roam.

Whispers of winter dance on the air,
Each flake a promise, soft as a prayer.
Beneath the vast sky, dreams take flight,
Lost in the splendor of pure, soft light.

Footprints emerge on a path so bright,
Stories unfold in the arms of night.
Cold breath mingles with laughter and cheer,
A moment of magic, the world draws near.

Trees wear jewels, glistening with frost,
In this quiet beauty, we count what's lost.
Yet hope springs anew with every dawn,
For in every heart, a song lives on.

So linger awhile, beneath the stars' glow,
In a shimmering world, let your heart flow.
A canvas of white, so tranquil, so vast,
Captured in time, a memory to last.

Hibernation's Embrace

In the heart of winter, life slows down,
Beneath thick blankets, the earth wears a frown.
Creatures nestle in their cozy homes,
Dreaming of spring when the sunlight roams.

The world outside, a frozen scene,
Bare branches reach for what once had been.
Silence wraps tightly, a comforting shroud,
While nature rests softly under a cloud.

Time passes slow in this slumbering phase,
As each flake of snow brings a peaceful gaze.
Within the stillness, seeds stir with might,
Awaiting the call of the warm daylight.

So let us embrace this stillness to share,
To find warmth in moments, create heartfelt care.
For in hibernation, our spirits renew,
Resting in silence, we linger anew.

In shadows of rest, we find love's own grace,
Nestled together in hibernation's embrace.
The world waits patiently, calm as the sea,
For life's vibrant pulse to awaken in me.

Fragments of Light on Chilled Pathways

Beneath the lamplight, shadows dance,
On chilled pathways, a fleeting glance.
Each step whispers secrets of old,
In the shimmering night, stories unfold.

Frost clings gently to the edges of dreams,
Echoing laughter, or so it seems.
Wrapped in warmth, yet feeling so bare,
Fragments of light in the crisp night air.

Footprints align in perfect rhythm,
As if the past offers wisdom.
The chill bites lightly, a kiss on the skin,
Guiding the wanderer patiently within.

Glimmers of stars punctuate the deep,
Awakening thoughts that we long to keep.
Like diamonds scattered on black velvet skies,
Hope reflects brightly from weeping eyes.

So roam these pathways, let spirits soar,
In the fragments of light, ancient lore.
Chilled whispers of night cradle all fears,
As magic unfolds and time disappears.

Celestial Frost and Wandering Thoughts

Beneath the canopy of night divine,
Celestial frost weaves a delicate line.
Thoughts drift like snowflakes in the sphere,
Wanderers lost with nothing to fear.

The moon whispers softly above the ground,
Guiding sweet secrets, a mystical sound.
In the stillness, we breathe in the cold,
While tales of old in our hearts unfold.

Stars twinkle gently, a celestial dance,
Inviting our spirits to take a chance.
In the embrace of the chill, we find peace,
A solace that offers a sweet release.

Let wandering thoughts in the winter bloom,
Sprout like flowers dispelling the gloom.
In the magic of night, we close our eyes,
Dreaming of worlds where the heart never lies.

So take a moment, reflect on the night,
Let frost paint dreams in shimmering light.
With celestial frost, let your spirit soar,
In wandering thoughts, we discover the more.

Night sings in the Language of Snow

In quiet woods where shadows play,
The snowflakes dance in soft array.
Whispers glide on the crisp night air,
As stars twinkle with silver flare.

Each flake a tale from the skies,
A hush that falls as daylight dies.
Moonlight bathes the world in glow,
While nature sighs in the language of snow.

Silent footsteps mark the ground,
In this enchanted night unbound.
The trees draped in white stand tall,
Listening to the night's soft call.

A world adorned in quiet grace,
Where dreams and winter's chill embrace.
With every breath, the night sings clear,
The beauty of a season here.

Softly, softly, the night unfolds,
In gentle whispers, the magic molds.
Wrapped in warmth from the cold outside,
The heart finds peace in winter's tide.

Luminescent Veil of Winter's Magic

A tapestry of shimmering white,
Cloaks the earth in pure delight.
Glowing softly beneath the moon,
Winter weaves her tender tune.

Each breath forms a cloud, sweet and bright,
In this stillness, all feels right.
With every flake that kisses ground,
A silent joy in beauty found.

Branches whisper secrets old,
In the chill, stories unfold.
The night unfolds a velvet hue,
As dreams come forth, draped anew.

Stars glisten like diamonds rare,
In this winter wonder, beyond compare.
A luminescent veil ignites,
Illuminating these frosty nights.

With every step, the magic flows,
In the glow of winter kisses those.
A soft embrace of flurries bright,
In the heart of the tranquil night.

Auroras Paint the Frozen Sky

Beneath the heavens, colors swirl,
As auroras dance, their ribbons twirl.
A canvas bright of green and gold,
Each stroke a wonder to behold.

The frozen sky, a world unseen,
Where light and magic weave between.
Whispers call from icy shores,
As nature opens her secret doors.

Stars gaze down with jealous glow,
As night unveils the cosmic show.
The breath of winter paints the scene,
As dreams take flight in realms serene.

In every flicker, stories rise,
Life dances under the shifting skies.
With colors bright, our spirits soar,
In the beauty of the night we explore.

Each moment fleeting, yet divine,
The auroras twist, like verses rhyme.
With every glance, the heart ignites,
A tapestry of wondrous sights.

Tales Spun from Frigid Whispers

In the quiet, secrets wane,
Frigid whispers form a refrain.
Through the trees, a story flows,
Of winter's heart, the hush bestows.

Frosted branches, tales unfold,
In whispers soft, where dreams are told.
A silent vow beneath the frost,
In the stillness, we find what's lost.

Echoes of laughter ride the breeze,
Of children dancing with joyful ease.
Each step a mystery, cold yet warm,
In winter's embrace, we find life's charm.

Moonlit nights hold secrets deep,
While nature's lullabies softly creep.
In every flake, a story lies,
Whispered soft 'neath the starry skies.

Tales spun of winter's graceful art,
In hushed tones, they fill the heart.
A magical world where dreams are near,
In frigid whispers, winter's cheer.

Quietude Beneath the Snows

Whispers of silence, soft and light,
A blanket of white, covering night.
Footsteps muffled, dreams unfold,
In peaceful moments, a story told.

Each flake a secret, drifting slow,
A gentle embrace from the heavens below.
Trees wear their gowns, pearly and pure,
While time stands still, serene and sure.

The world is a canvas, blank and wide,
With strokes of frost, nature's pride.
In this respite, hearts take flight,
Finding solace in the quiet night.

Beneath the moon's watchful gaze,
Life lingers softly, lost in a daze.
Frozen gardens, a tranquil grace,
In stillness, we find our place.

Snowflakes gather, a soft refrain,
Carving beauty through the mundane.
In winter's glow, warmth we find,
Quietude lingers, gently entwined.

Frozen Echoes

In the stillness, echoes call,
Whispers of winter, soft and small.
Memories linger where shadows play,
In the heart of frost, they sway.

Beneath the ice, time holds tight,
Frozen moments in pale moonlight.
Each sound a shiver, a breath of air,
Lost in the silence, floating with care.

Crystal branches, glistening bright,
Reflecting the dawn, a fleeting sight.
Nature's breath, a gentle sigh,
In frozen echoes, dreams fly high.

Cold winds whisper through the trees,
Songs of winter on the breeze.
A tapestry woven with each frost,
Reminders of what may be lost.

Yet in the chill, warmth can bloom,
Hope flickers softly, dispelling gloom.
Each echo a promise, softly it grows,
In the realm of the frozen, our spirit glows.

Beneath the Frost

Underneath the frost, life awaits,
Hidden beneath winter's gates.
Roots entwined in the cold earth's hold,
Secrets of spring yet to unfold.

The stillness blankets where warmth once lay,
Nature sleeps, dreaming of day.
Icicles shimmer, a silvery thread,
Guarding the whispers of things unsaid.

In the hush of the morn, hope ignites,
As sunlight rises and banishes nights.
Each thaw a reminder, life's embrace,
Beneath the frost, we find our place.

Silent promises in the crisp air,
Tenderness wrapped in winter's care.
With every heartbeat, nature holds tight,
The promise of spring in the depth of night.

So let us wander where shadows blend,
And find the beauty that frost can transcend.
In every season, a tale to share,
Beneath the frost, life waits there.

Lanterns in the Dark

In the deep of night, lanterns glow,
Guiding lost souls where shadows go.
A flicker of hope, a dance of light,
Casting warmth in the chill of night.

Beneath the stars, stories unfold,
Each lantern a tale, each flame bold.
Whispers of dreams, softly ignited,
In the heart of darkness, hope is invited.

The pathway glimmers, leading us on,
Through valleys of silence, till the dawn.
With courage, we travel through shadows cast,
Each step a memory, each moment vast.

In the luminescence, fears dissipate,
Guided by lanterns, we illuminate fate.
Together we wander, hand in hand,
As love lights the way, like grains of sand.

So fear not the dark; let the glow be your guide,
For within the shadows, dreams abide.
With lanterns burning, spirits rise,
In the depths of night, the heart never lies.

Celestial Blankets and Starlit Shadows

In gentle night, the stars descend,
A tapestry where dreams extend.
Whispers of light in silence weave,
As shadows dance, our hearts believe.

The sky's embrace, a soft cocoon,
Each twinkle sings a tender tune.
Celestial blankets drape the land,
In starlit shadows, hand in hand.

A silver glow on tranquil seas,
Where wishes float upon the breeze.
The universe, a boundless art,
In cosmic realms, we find our heart.

As night unfolds, the world is still,
In quietude, we feel the thrill.
Celestial wonders, vast and bright,
Guide us through the velvet night.

When dawn approaches, softly clear,
Starlit shadows gradually disappear.
Yet in our hearts, their warmth remains,
Celestial blankets, love's sweet chains.

Frost-kissed Whispers in the Dark

In winter's breath, the world does sigh,
Frost-kissed whispers, low and high.
The moon glows softly on the trees,
A lullaby carried by the breeze.

Each flake a gem, unique, divine,
Painting paths with a glimmering line.
Beneath the stars, our secrets shared,
In quiet darkness, hearts are bared.

Silvery shadows drape the ground,
In frozen stillness, joy is found.
A world transformed, serene and bright,
Frost-kissed whispers in the night.

With every breath, the air is crisp,
In nature's arms, we gently lisp.
Softly we tread, as dreams take flight,
In the embrace of cold delight.

As dawn approaches, shadows fade,
But frosty whispers won't evade.
In every heart, their stories blend,
A winter's tale that has no end.

A Lullaby for the Winter Moon

Beneath the stars, the moon's embrace,
A lullaby in stillness space.
Soft silver beams on blankets white,
Caress the world, a soothing light.

The winter whispers through the trees,
A melody that stirs the breeze.
As shadows dance, we close our eyes,
And dream beneath the quiet skies.

A gentle hush, the night unfolds,
A thousand stories yet untold.
Each silver ray, a soft caress,
A lullaby, sweet, to bless.

The world sleeps deep, in peace it lies,
As winter moon ascends the skies.
In dreams we wander, wild and free,
To tune with nature's symphony.

Though morning comes and dreams may wane,
The lullaby will still remain.
In every heart, its notes will play,
A song of night, a bright array.

The Stillness of Fallen Hues

In autumn's grasp, the leaves descend,
A tapestry where colors blend.
Golden whispers kiss the ground,
In stillness, nature's peace is found.

A carpet rich in crimson glow,
The earth adorned in nature's show.
With each soft breeze, a gentle sigh,
As fallen hues wave their goodbye.

The trees stand tall, their branches bare,
Embracing change with tender care.
In this quiet, hearts align,
With the stillness, we softly entwine.

Beneath the sky, a canvas grand,
Fallen hues hold every hand.
In silence deep, the stories bloom,
Of seasons past in twilight's room.

As winter nears and colors fade,
A memory of warmth is made.
In the stillness, hope will arise,
For spring awaits under gray skies.

Nighthaze in the Pines

Shadows dance beneath the trees,
Moonlight weaves through gentle leaves,
Whispers drift on midnight air,
Secrets linger, soft and rare.

Branches sway with quiet grace,
Nature holds a sacred space,
Stars above begin to gleam,
In the hush, we feel the dream.

Cool breeze wraps the twilight night,
Echoes chase the fading light,
Each breath stirs the hidden deep,
In this moment, silence we keep.

Time stands still as shadows grow,
In the pines, where soft winds blow,
A symphony of subtle sound,
In this beauty, we are bound.

Nighthaze cloaks the world in peace,
Whispers of the pines increase,
Underneath the cosmic glow,
In the stillness, hearts will know.

Whispering Winds

Gentle breezes, soft and shy,
Carry tales from far and nigh,
Rustling leaves speak low and sweet,
In their dance, our dreams will meet.

Winds that wander, winds that play,
Guide the night into the day,
Every sigh and silent plea,
Echoes in eternity.

Murmurs thrumming through the trees,
Telling stories with the breeze,
Each caress upon the skin,
Brings the warmth of love within.

Whispering winds, our faithful friends,
Calling forth as daylight ends,
Nurturing the hope we find,
In the softness, hearts unwind.

In the twilight, breezes weave,
Weaving dreams that we believe,
With each pulse, the world aligns,
In sweet harmony, it shines.

Cold Embrace

In the stillness of the night,
Frosty breath, a silver light,
Nature sleeps with whispered sighs,
Underneath the starry skies.

Every flake that falls so near,
Curtains winter's chill with cheer,
Biting wind that wraps around,
In this hush, a soothing sound.

Branches wear a crown of white,
Wonders frozen, pure and bright,
In the quiet, beauty swells,
As the clutch of winter dwells.

Cold embrace, a tender hold,
Stories of the past retold,
Memories in crisp air breathe,
In the quiet, hearts believe.

With each moment, time stands still,
Embracing winter's ghostly thrill,
In the chill, we find our place,
Bound together in cold embrace.

Starlight Over Frozen Fields

In the darkness, starlight glows,
Illuminating all it knows,
Fields of silver, pure and wide,
Underneath the cosmic tide.

Frosted grains that shimmer bright,
Catch the gaze of endless night,
Every twinkle whispers dreams,
Flowing softly like moonbeams.

Footsteps crunch on icy ground,
In this place, peace can be found,
Nature's art, a tranquil scene,
Bathed in silver, pure and keen.

Stars above, like diamonds fall,
In their light, we hear the call,
Frozen fields, where silence reigns,
In the stillness, calm sustains.

In this moment, heart takes flight,
With the magic of the night,
Starlit dreams and winter's breath,
In their beauty, we find depth.

Echoes in a Wintry Landscape

Whispers dance upon the breeze,
Footprints vanish 'neath the snow.
Trees stand tall in frozen ease,
Time slips by, soft and slow.

Moonlight casts a silver sheen,
Blankets wrap the world in white.
Shadows glimpse what once has been,
Secrets kept within the night.

Cold winds sing a haunting song,
As stars blink in the dark sky.
Along the path where dreams belong,
Memories echo, soft and shy.

Frosted breath in crystal air,
Nature's stillness grips the hour.
Every moment, crystal rare,
Holds within a fleeting power.

In this realm of frozen grace,
Solitude finds its gentle plea.
Each echo leaves a quiet trace,
In the heart of winter's sea.

Luminous Nights in an Icy Embrace

Stars ignite the velvet skies,
Over fields of sparkling snow.
Each breath whispers, soft goodbyes,
As the night begins to glow.

Candles flicker in the dark,
Casting warmth with gentle light.
Frosty petals leave their mark,
On the canvas of the night.

In this deep and tranquil hush,
Hearts align with nature's beat.
Silence dances, soft and lush,
Time retreats in pure retreat.

Crystals shimmer on the ground,
Fairy tales begin to weave.
In the quiet, peace is found,
A comforting web to believe.

Underneath the moon's soft gaze,
Dreams unfold with every glance.
In the heart's most secret maze,
Hope ignites a shivering dance.

Starlit Paths Through Powdered Dreams

Footsteps whisper on the ground,
In a land of silver light.
Where the magic can be found,
Underneath the stars so bright.

Dreams awaken in the chill,
As the night begins to play.
Windsong weaves a gentle thrill,
In the twilight's soft array.

Each flake falls with whispered grace,
Draping all in glistening white.
Time is lost in frozen space,
Held within the starry light.

In this place of quiet thought,
Heartbeats echo like a song.
Every moment dearly sought,
Keeps the night where it belongs.

Powdered dreams on starlit trails,
Guide us through the ether's glow.
In this world where magic sails,
Let our spirits freely flow.

Adrift in a Silent Polar Sea

Waves of crystal, calm and still,
Echoes of the sea's soft breath.
In this silence, hearts fulfill,
Whispers dance with shades of death.

Icebergs rise like ancient dreams,
Guardians of the cold, wild night.
The horizon softly gleams,
As stars twinkle, pure and bright.

In this endless icy flow,
Time is lost, a gentle sigh.
Every shadow, every glow,
Calls for longing, draws us nigh.

Through the thick and biting air,
Hope unfurls its fragile wings.
In this realm beyond all care,
Nature's song eternally sings.

Each heartbeat syncs with the tide,
As our souls drift on the sea.
In the stillness, love's our guide,
In this vast infinity.

The Silver Gown of Mother Nature

The silver gown flows down the hill,
Draped in whispers of the chill.
Each tree adorned, a crystal sight,
Embracing nature, pure delight.

The streams are frozen, whispers cease,
In quiet moments, find your peace.
Beneath the stars, a gentle glow,
Nature's beauty, a stunning show.

The mountains wear their icy crown,
As the world sleeps, wrapped in brown.
A silent grace, the air so still,
The silver gown, a heart to fill.

Amongst the pines, the shadows play,
In this moment, night holds sway.
Nature's breath, a tender sigh,
In the silver gown, dreams can fly.

The dawn will come, the frost will fade,
Yet in our hearts, the memory laid.
Of Mother Nature, draped in white,
Her silver gown, a pure delight.

Memories Lost in Winter's Grasp

Faint echoes linger, softly call,
In winter's grasp, we feel it all.
The laughter fades, the warmth recedes,
In snow-covered fields, silence breeds.

Footprints buried beneath the snow,
Where once we danced, now whispers flow.
Moments lost in the frosty night,
In every flake, a tale takes flight.

The memories shimmer like ice on trees,
Fragrant whispers in the frozen breeze.
A journey mapped by seasons past,
In winter's grip, they seem to last.

Yet as we walk on frozen ground,
Lost memories in silence found.
The heart remembers, though time may fade,
In winter's grasp, sweet loves conveyed.

So let us cherish the cold embrace,
For every loss, there is a trace.
In winter's grasp, we hold it tight,
Memories formed in tranquil night.

Night's Soft Cradle of Snowflakes

In night's soft cradle, snowflakes play,
They dance and tumble, swirl away.
Each flake a whisper from the sky,
In silence where the shadows lie.

The world is hushed, a blanket white,
Under the warmth of gentle night.
Stars peek down through curtain's fold,
A winter's tale, in dreams retold.

Glow of moonlight paints the scene,
Amongst the trees, a twinkling sheen.
A fleeting moment, soft and pure,
Within this beauty, we endure.

Snowflakes rest on quiet lips,
Kissing the world with icy tips.
In night's embrace, we find our peace,
As time stands still, our worries cease.

So let us wander through this night,
With hearts aglow, in winter's light.
Each flake a dream, a secret told,
In night's soft cradle, we are whole.

Silence Wrapped in Whiteness

Wrapped in whiteness, silence reigns,
Nature whispers, free from chains.
Each snow-draped branch, a gentle sigh,
In peace we rest, as time slips by.

The world asleep in snowy grace,
A tranquil heart finds its place.
Where once was chaos, now it's calm,
Within the hush, a simple balm.

In every flake, a story spun,
Of fleeting moments, now begun.
The air is crisp, the stars so bright,
In silence wrapped, we feel the light.

So linger here, beneath the sky,
In quiet wonder, let us lie.
For in this stillness, we hold tight,
A kindred spirit, day and night.

Wrapped in whiteness, dreams will soar,
In silence, we find so much more.
A world reborn, with every breath,
In this stillness, life and death.

A Veil of Frost on Sleeping Earth

A quiet hush wraps round the ground,
With silver blankets, soft and round.
Trees wear coats of glistening white,
As stars above twinkle in the night.

Footprints frozen in glimmering snow,
Whispers of dreams where warm winds blow.
Each breath a cloud, both light and frail,
Nature's magic, a frosty veil.

In this stillness, time stands still,
Winter's breath a gentle chill.
The world adorned in icy lace,
Holds the secrets of this place.

Moonlight dances on fields so bright,
Painting shadows, crafting light.
With every flake that drifts and sways,
The earth sleeps on through winter's days.

As dawn breaks gentle, the frost will fade,
Yet in this moment, enchantments laid.
A timeless tale the cold winds tell,
Of a veil of frost where dreams dwell.

Cold Caresses of Winter's Night

The night descends in a shroud of gray,
Whispers of winter softly play.
Moonbeams lace the barren trees,
Carrying echoes on the breeze.

Each breath taken, a plume of white,
Frosted lawns in the dimming light.
Stars emerge, a shimmering sight,
As shadows stretch in winter's night.

The world is hushed, as if in prayer,
Listening close to the crisp cold air.
A tranquil pause, a moment rare,
Winter's embrace, a tender care.

With every flake that flutters down,
A sparkling crown on nature's crown.
The chill wraps round like a soothing quilt,
In the quiet hours where dreams are built.

And as the night gives way to dawn,
The beauty lingers, though cold is gone.
Each heartbeat marks the passage bright,
Of cold caresses in winter's night.

Echoes of Solitude in the Chill

Amidst the cold, the shadows creep,
Where silence reigns, and secrets sleep.
Each breath a ghost, a fleeting sigh,
In winter's realm, where dreams lie high.

The trees stand tall, their branches bare,
Holding stories in the frosty air.
Echoes linger in the chill,
Of memories soft, and quiet will.

Footfalls muffled on the frozen ground,
Nature's symphony, a whispering sound.
In solitude, we find our peace,
As the world around us takes its lease.

With every gust, the night unfolds,
Tales of sorrows, the heart beholds.
The chill carries voices long unheard,
Of solitude's grace, a gentle word.

As dawn approaches, light will spill,
On echoes of solitude in the chill.
The sun will rise, and warmth will bloom,
Yet winter's whispers softly loom.

Gentle Murmurs in the Silent Wind

In the stillness, whispers blend,
Gentle murmurs, the night transcends.
Branches sway in soft caress,
Holding secrets of wilderness.

The silent wind knows every tale,
From soaring peaks to the quiet vale.
Each breeze that stirs the amber leaves,
Cradles dreams that the night weaves.

Moonlight bathes the earth in grace,
Illuminating each hidden space.
The world feels close, yet far away,
In nature's hold, we long to stay.

Frosted whispers through the air sweep,
Promises made beneath the deep.
As night lingers, we close our eyes,
To gentle murmurs and starlit skies.

With morning light, the whispers fade,
Yet still, in heart, their songs are laid.
For in the night, we find and lend,
Gentle murmurs that never end.

Frosted Footsteps

In the morning light, crisp and bright,
Footprints linger, a fleeting sight.
Blankets of white on the ground untold,
Whispers of winter, a magic so bold.

Trees wear their coats, heavy with frost,
Every branch glimmers, nothing is lost.
Nature's embrace in an icy hold,
Stories of seasons, in silence, unfold.

Breath of the chill in the frozen air,
Moments of wonder, a world so rare.
Every step echoing beneath the sun,
Frosted footprints, the journey's begun.

Winds gently hum, a lullaby sweet,
Guiding the wanderer, soft on their feet.
The beauty of trails etched on the ground,
In the quiet of morning, serenity found.

Midnight's Canvas

Stars like diamonds against velvet night,
Brush strokes of darkness bathe the light.
Whispers of dreams float on the air,
Caught in the moment, suspended in care.

Moonbeams dance on shadows that play,
Silhouettes twirling, lost in the sway.
Colors of dusk merge with shadows deep,
A palette of whispers, secrets to keep.

Canvas of midnight, a masterpiece spun,
Each twinkle a story, each heartbeat a drum.
Painting the heavens with wishes and time,
A symphony's echo, a soft, gentle chime.

In the embrace of the quiet hour,
Dreams take flight, like petals from flower.
Each star a wish, in the dark they gleam,
Collecting our hopes, igniting our dream.

Serene Silence

In a world hushed, where whispers fade,
Calm drapes softly, a gentle cascade.
Nature holds breath, a moment of pause,
In the serene silence, the heart draws.

Mountains stand guard, cloaked in stillness,
Rivers flow gently, a dance of willfulness.
Clouds drift lazily across the blue,
Moments like these, pure and true.

In the quiet corners of a tranquil mind,
Peace like a river, steadily unwind.
Every heartbeat echoes the hush of the day,
In serene silence, worries drift away.

Time slows gracefully, a lingering sigh,
The beauty of now, a sweet lullaby.
Wrapped in the comfort of stillness so deep,
In gentle embrace, we surrender to sleep.

Frostbitten Wishes

Under the stars, where frostflowers bloom,
Wishes take flight in the cold of the gloom.
Whispers of dreams on the winter's breath,
Carved in the ice, a dance with death.

Frostbitten fingers clutching the night,
Hoping for warmth, an ember of light.
Each wish a spark in the deepening cold,
Stories of hopes and fears, untold.

Silent reflections on a frozen stream,
We cast our desires, igniting the dream.
In the heart of the chill, we yearn for the fire,
Frostbitten wishes, fueled by desire.

As dawn breaks in gold, the icy grip fades,
Dreams melt away in the sunlight's cascades.
Yet in the cold, we'll remember this night,
Frostbitten wishes, ignited by light.

Shadows on White

Frosty whispers in the air,
Softly blanketing the ground,
Footprints lost without a care,
Ghosts of silence all around.

Trees stand tall, a frozen row,
Casting shadows, long and deep,
Nature's quiet, gentle show,
As the earth drifts into sleep.

Moonlight dances on the snow,
Glinting silver, pure and bright,
In this world, time moves so slow,
Wrapped in peaceful, wondrous night.

Echoes fade, the stillness grows,
Every breath a tale untold,
In this realm where beauty flows,
Warmth within the frigid cold.

Quiet hearts and watching eyes,
Find the magic here tonight,
In the hush where spirit flies,
Lost in shadows, bathed in light.

Hushed Wilderness

In the heart of untamed lands,
Nature whispers soft and low,
Trees like guardians take their stands,
Where wild rivers calmly flow.

Moonlit paths through ancient woods,
Silhouettes of branches sway,
Echoes travel, sweetly good,
Guiding lost souls on their way.

Underneath a blanket bright,
Stars emerge, a shimmering quilt,
Filling darkness with their light,
In this peace, all fears are spilt.

Gentle breezes kiss the leaves,
Carrying secrets from afar,
Nature's song, a tune that weaves,
Catching wishes on a star.

In this hushed, untouched domain,
Life awakens, dreams take flight,
In the wild, we feel no pain,
Just a promise of delight.

Stars Above the Drifts

Beneath the vast, eternal sky,
The night unfolds its velvet seam,
As silver stars in silence sigh,
Guiding wanderers in dreams.

Mounded drifts of glistening snow,
Cradle secrets, still, and white,
Winds that whisper, soft and low,
Stirring magic with their might.

A cosmic dance of light unfolds,
Painting stories on the night,
Each twinkle holds a truth untold,
Filling hearts with pure delight.

Footsteps trace the frozen ground,
Hearts aglow with dreams so bright,
In this landscape, peace is found,
Beneath the stars, pure and right.

Here we pause, and time stands still,
Each breath a thread of connection,
In the quiet, dreams fulfill,
Guided by the stars' perfection.

Enchanted Stillness

In the garden where thoughts can roam,
Every petal sings a song,
Here we find our hearts a home,
In stillness, where we belong.

Whispers float on gentle air,
Rustling leaves tell tales of peace,
In this moment, nothing's rare,
Time and troubles find release.

The twilight casts a golden hue,
Bathing secrets in its glow,
As shadows dance, the world feels new,
In this haven, love will grow.

Stars emerge, like dreams in flight,
Glimmers of hope in the night sky,
In the deep, soft, tender light,
We'll find solace, you and I.

As silence wraps the world in grace,
We hold each other, hand in hand,
In the stillness, we embrace,
In this enchanted, timeless land.

Gentle Flurries

Softly drifting from the clouds,
Whispers dance through the still night,
Covering Earth like a tender shroud,
Blanketing shadows in purest white.

Frosty patterns on window panes,
Nature's artwork, serene and bright,
Silent joy that remains,
In the hush of the moonlight.

Each flake tells a story yet untold,
Secrets carried on the breeze,
A magical touch in winter's hold,
Bringing comfort and quiet peace.

Winds of winter softly blow,
Trees adorned in sparkling glow,
Gentle flurries weave their spell,
As nightingale bids the day farewell.

In this moment, all feels right,
Hearts are warmed by chilly air,
Glistening beneath soft starlight,
Gentle flurries, beyond compare.

Glistening Dreams

In the twilight's gentle embrace,
Dreams awaken and take flight,
Like stars scattered in a vast space,
Glistening softly, pure delight.

Whispers of hopes like candle flames,
Flicker gently in the night,
Eager hearts calling out names,
Painting visions, bold and bright.

Through silken clouds, visions flow,
Mirrored in the moon's soft gleam,
Illuminating paths we sow,
Guiding us through every dream.

In the stillness, fears dissolve,
With every heartbeat, tales unfold,
A tapestry of life's resolve,
Weaving stories yet untold.

In glistening dreams, we're set free,
Floating lightly on soft wings,
Boundless realms await to see,
The magic that dreaming brings.

Ghosts of Winter

Silent whispers in the cold,
Echoes of lives long past,
Cloaked in white, the stories told,
Ghosts of winter, shadows cast.

Frosty breath of ancient days,
Memories linger, soft and low,
Through the trees, a haunting haze,
Wanders through the silent snow.

Each flake that falls, a soul that's free,
Dancing lightly in the air,
Embracing all we dare not see,
The warmth of love, forever rare.

In the moon's pale, watchful eye,
Ghostly trails begin to weave,
Carrying whispers to the sky,
In winter's chill, we believe.

As night descends on wintry fields,
The past and present intertwine,
In each breath, the heart reveals,
Ghosts of winter, forever shine.

Echoes in the Snow

Footsteps crunch on winter's ground,
Memories tread upon the white,
Each sound a whisper all around,
Echoes linger in the night.

Beneath the blanket, softly laid,
Stories buried, dreams concealed,
The magic of the night cascade,
In the stillness, truth revealed.

Frosted branches sway and bend,
Echoes of laughter fill the air,
Moments shared that do not end,
In the quiet, love laid bare.

Ghostly figures, shadows dance,
In the glow of twilight's grace,
A perfect, fleeting kind of chance,
To trace the past in time and space.

As dawn approaches, colors blend,
The frozen world begins to glow,
Echoes linger, hearts transcend,
Embrace the beauty of the snow.

Crisp Air and Still Hearts

In the morning light, we stand still,
Breath visible, our hopes fulfill.
Nature whispers, soft and clear,
Crisp air around, all we hold dear.

Leaves crunch beneath our quiet feet,
With every step, our hearts repeat.
Moments captured, time slows down,
In this stillness, we're unbound.

Sky painted blue, a canvas bright,
We walk together, hearts in flight.
The chill embraces, warm we stay,
In each other's gaze, we find our way.

Sunlight breaks, shadows align,
Hand in hand, we glide and twine.
Crisp air wraps us, love's sweet call,
In this moment, we have it all.

With open hearts and dreams that soar,
What lies ahead, we can't ignore.
But in this present, all feels right,
Crisp air and still, the world ignites.

Veils of Ice

Across the lake, a shimmering sight,
Veils of ice catch the fading light.
Whispers of winter dance on air,
A hidden world, both cold and rare.

Branches adorned with crystal lace,
Nature's artistry, a frozen grace.
Footsteps echo in the silent chill,
A tranquil moment, time stands still.

Glistening surfaces beneath the sun,
Mirrored dreams of what's begun.
We traverse this wintery land,
With hopes entwined, together we stand.

Clouds drift by in a pastel sweep,
Secrets held in the icy deep.
Every breath releases a sigh,
In this beauty, we learn to fly.

Veils of ice, a fleeting phase,
Captured in these wintry days.
Hold this moment, let it stay,
In frozen time, we find our way.

Night Chilled Reverie

Beneath the stars, the world feels small,
Whispers echo, shadows call.
Moonlight bathes the earth in glow,
In night chilled reverie, we flow.

The trees stand tall, their silence wise,
As constellations dance in the skies.
We share our dreams, a gentle sigh,
In this moment, time slips by.

Cold air wraps us in tender embrace,
Two hearts align in this sacred space.
Every glance ignites the night,
In your presence, the world feels right.

Footsteps echo on the frozen ground,
With every heartbeat, love's profound.
In chilled air, our spirits rise,
In the reverie, we find our ties.

As night deepens, quiet falls,
In the stillness, passion calls.
Night chilled whispers, soft and sweet,
Together forever, our hearts will meet.

Silhouette of Peace

Sunset glows with a gentle hue,
Casting shadows, a tranquil view.
In the evening calm, we stand apart,
Silhouette of peace, a work of art.

Colors blend in twilight's kiss,
In this silence, we find our bliss.
Soft whispers echo in the air,
A moment of stillness, a silent prayer.

Stars emerge in the darkening sky,
We share our dreams, as time drifts by.
In the dusk, our hearts take flight,
In the silhouette, we find our light.

Collecting moments, love's embrace,
In this stillness, we find our place.
The world fades, just you and me,
In this silhouette, we feel so free.

As night envelops, peace resides,
With every heartbeat, love abides.
In the shadows, where dreams unfold,
A silhouette of peace, a story told.

Moonlit Solitude

In the still of night, I wander free,
Beneath the glow of the silver sea.
Whispers of dreams in the gentle breeze,
A silent song that puts my heart at ease.

Stars above twinkle with a bright embrace,
Illuminating shadows, a soft, warm grace.
Steps echo softly on the path I roam,
In moonlit solitude, I find my home.

The world sleeps deep, wrapped in night's soft shroud,
Yet here I stand, quiet, calm, and proud.
Each flicker of light dances in my mind,
A tapestry of thoughts so intertwined.

I breathe in peace as the world drifts away,
In this sacred hush where feelings sway.
No voice but mine in this tranquil space,
A moment held in time, a sweet embrace.

As dawn draws near, with a soft, warm sigh,
I bid farewell to the starry sky.
In the heart of night, I found my heart,
In moonlit solitude, I played my part.

Chill of Forgotten Paths

Through twisted woods where shadows creep,
I walk the paths where memories sleep.
The chill of night wraps around my soul,
A haunting echo, a whispering toll.

Footsteps tread upon the frozen ground,
In silence deep, no voice, no sound.
Branches stretch like skeletal hands,
Reaching for secrets in forgotten lands.

A fog enshrouds the weary trail,
As darkness weaves its mournful veil.
Lost in thoughts of what was once bright,
In the chill of forgotten paths, I take flight.

Each breath I draw crystallizes the air,
A memory lingers, steeped in despair.
But hope glimmers like the faintest star,
Guiding me onward, no matter how far.

Yet in this gloom, resilience wakes,
A spirit unbroken; it softly breaks.
I'll find my way, though the shadows bind,
In the chill of forgotten paths, I'm unconfined.

Dusk in the Abyss

As daylight fades into the dark abyss,
A shroud of mystery, a fleeting kiss.
The horizon blushes, soft hues blend,
In the twilight where the shadows send.

Colors swirl in a tempestuous flow,
Where dreams and fears intertwine and grow.
Each heartbeat echoes the silent fight,
In the deepening dusk that swallows light.

Stars peer down with a watchful gaze,
Amongst the chaos, they set ablaze.
I walk through whispers, the night's embrace,
In the abyss where I dare to face.

The chill of night wraps tight around,
Yet in this vast, I am spellbound.
A bridge of silence holds my hand,
As hope ignites in this shadowed land.

Dusk may linger, yet I remain brave,
A soul unyielding, my heart a wave.
In the depth of darkness, I find my way,
Through dusk in the abyss, I'll not dismay.

Frost Over Silent Woods

In winter's grip, the world stands still,
A frosty blanket, white and chill.
Trees adorned in crystal lace,
Silent woods wear a quiet face.

Footprints crunch on the frozen ground,
In this serene, enchanted sound.
Nature's breath held in frigid air,
A moment of peace, perfect and rare.

Each branch trembles with the weight of frost,
Memories linger of warmth embossed.
In shadows cast by the pale moonlight,
The woods awaken with whispers slight.

As stars twinkle in the darkened sky,
The stillness beckons, a gentle sigh.
Beneath the frost, life waits to bloom,
In silent woods, dispelling gloom.

When spring arrives, with a vibrant kiss,
These woods will echo with joyous bliss.
But for now, in winter's tender hold,
Frost over silent woods speaks untold.

Winter's Whisper

When snowflakes fall like whispers light,
The world is cloaked in purest white.
Each breath a cloud that swiftly flies,
Underneath the gray, muted skies.

Branches bow with icy grace,
Nature wears a quiet face.
Echoes of the forest hold,
Stories wrapped in frost and cold.

A silent night, the stars so bright,
Dance above in glimmering sight.
The chill that bites, it softly sings,
Of dreams that winter always brings.

Footsteps crunch on snowy ground,
Lost in thoughts that swirl around.
The air is crisp, the silence deep,
In winter's arms, the world will sleep.

A fleeting touch of day must part,
As twilight holds a frosty heart.
Underneath the silver glow,
Whispers of winter softly flow.

Frosted Silence

In the stillness of the night,
Frosted breath gives life a bite.
Nature hushed, a breath held tight,
Wrapped in blankets, pure delight.

Branches draped in icy lace,
A quiet dance, a slow embrace.
Snowflakes tumble without sound,
Carpet soft on frozen ground.

Footprints mark the way we tread,
Whispers echo, softly spread.
Every heartbeat, a gentle thrum,
In this world, we quietly come.

Stars above like diamonds gleam,
Reflecting on the frozen stream.
A moment caught, forever stays,
In frosted silence, time decays.

Gathered 'round the warm embrace,
We find solace in this space.
Silent breaths, we softly trace,
In frost's soft touch, we find our place.

Glinting Icicles

Icicles hang from eaves with grace,
Glistening like jewels in their place.
Sunlight dances on their edge,
Nature's art, a frigid pledge.

Each drip a note of time's own song,
Marking where the moments belong.
With winter's breath, they shimmer bright,
Capturing the fleeting light.

Beneath them, shadows softly play,
In this icy grand ballet.
The crisp air sings a frosty tune,
Beneath the watchful, ghostly moon.

Children laugh in the snow below,
Building dreams where cold winds blow.
They watch the beauties overhead,
In awe of what the ice has bred.

As winter wanes and melts away,
The icicles weep, a soft decay.
Yet memories of their brilliant glow,
Will linger long, though seasons flow.

Moonlit Blankets

Beneath the moon's soft, silver light,
The world transforms, a wondrous sight.
Cloaked in blankets of soft white,
The silence sings of winter's night.

Stars embroidered in the sky,
Whispering secrets from on high.
Each twinkle tells a tale of old,
While dreams of warmth and love unfold.

The trees stand tall, in coats of frost,
Their branches heavy, beauty lost.
Yet in their stillness, strength resides,
In quiet solitude, they bide.

Footsteps soft on snow-kissed ground,
Following echoes that surround.
In moonlit night, we find our peace,
Where all our worries gently cease.

As winter weaves its magic spell,
In frosted beauty, we can dwell.
With each heartbeat, nature's lore,
We treasure nights that we adore.

The Dance of Shadows and Snowflakes

In twilight's fade, shadows play,
Snowflakes twirl in soft ballet.
Whispers blend with night's embrace,
Every flake finds its right place.

They drift lightly, soft and fair,
Chasing dreams through icy air.
A fleeting touch, so pure, divine,
In winter's arms, hearts intertwine.

Dancing moments swept away,
In the glow of moonlit sway.
Each shadow hides a tale untold,
In silvered light, magic unfolds.

Together they weave silent songs,
Echoing where the stillness throngs.
A harmony in night's cool breath,
Embracing life, defying death.

Footprints lost in crystal frost,
Connections made but never crossed.
Time stands still in this serene,
A fleeting world, both felt and seen.

A Dreamwalker's Journey on Cold Winds

Through the night, the dreamwalker roams,
On cold winds that whisper of homes.
With a heart that knows no bounds,
In the sky, lost hope resounds.

Each gust carries secrets anew,
Paths of stars and skies of blue.
In shadows deep, visions gleam,
Lost in the warmth of a dream.

Footsteps trace where others tread,
Following lines of words unsaid.
A realm where fantasies take flight,
Carried far on waves of night.

Through frozen fields and silver streams,
Beneath the weight of shattered dreams.
Awake or asleep, who can decide,
In the journey, hearts collide.

Like autumn leaves in swirling dance,
Fate can shift with a single glance.
As cold winds sway the shadows long,
The dreamwalker finds where they belong.

Portraits in White Beneath the Cedar

Beneath the cedar's timeless shade,
Portraits in white, nature's parade.
Sparse branches hold a snowy frame,
Every flake speaks a silent name.

Frozen whispers linger near,
In a world that feels so clear.
The beauty lies in the purest white,
Wrapped in a cloak of soft twilight.

Each footprint tells a secret plot,
A fleeting moment, not forgot.
As winter's palette paints the ground,
In its silence, solace found.

In every twist, a tale unfolds,
Of love and warmth, of hearts so bold.
Beneath the cedar's sheltering boughs,
Nature breathes, and time allows.

The chill that holds, the soft and bright,
Crafts portraits drawn from day to night.
Nature weaves its gentle art,
In every fray, it heals the heart.

Whispers of Night Carried on the Breeze

In the silence, secrets flow,
Whispers carried soft and low.
Through the trees, the stories glide,
In moonlit paths where dreams reside.

Each breeze a gentle, soothing sigh,
Holding wishes that float by.
Stars above, twinkling bright,
Guiding hearts through the night.

A tapestry of shadows spun,
Where the night and day are one.
Crisp air feels alive with sound,
In quiet places, magic found.

In hushed tones of a sleeping land,
Nature's lullabies gently stand.
While the world sleeps, spirits rise,
Beneath the cloak of starry skies.

With every breath, the night unspools,
A melody that softly cools.
Carried forth on whispers sweet,
Where dreams and nightingale hearts meet.

Veils of Winter's Breath

Veils of fog drape the trees,
Silent whispers ride the breeze.
A world wrapped in icy lace,
Each branch holds a delicate trace.

Footsteps crunch on the powdered ground,
Nature sleeps, yet life abounds.
The sun hides behind clouds so gray,
Yet hope breaks forth, come what may.

Frosty breath upon the air,
Beauty found in the stillness there.
With each flake that swirls and spins,
A soft reminder: winter begins.

Nights grow long in silent expanse,
Stars reflect a tranquil dance.
Beneath the moon's soft, silver glow,
Dreams awaken in the cold below.

The heart feels the chill in its beat,
Yet warmth flows in through the retreat.
For in this season, strong and bleak,
Life stirs softly in hushed mystique.

Nature's Frozen Lullaby

In the hush of evening's trail,
Snowflakes fall without fail.
Each shimmer like a forgotten sigh,
A soft song from the winter sky.

Whispers of trees in gentle dance,
Under the moon's entrancing glance.
Cradled in the arms of night,
Nature hums, serene and tight.

Crystal formations catch the light,
Painting shadows, delicate and slight.
A lullaby sung through the frost,
In this beauty, nothing's lost.

Branches bow with their heavy load,
Every pathway, a glittering road.
The world appears as a fairytale,
In winter's breath, hearts shall prevail.

Dreams weave through the icy air,
A gentle calm, a whispered prayer.
For in the stillness, magic lies,
Nature's lullaby never dies.

Star-Kissed Slumber

In the velvet of night's embrace,
Stars twinkle, a glowing trace.
Each spark a wish, so sweetly spun,
Casting dreams where daylight's done.

The world is hushed, a tranquil sigh,
Beneath the watchful cosmic eye.
Snow blankets all in quiet peace,
While worries of the day release.

Moonlight dances on frozen streams,
Stirring softly the heart's dreams.
A tapestry woven with stardust bright,
Wrapping the dark in gentle light.

Whispers of night sing soft and low,
Guiding souls where spirits flow.
Each breath a mystery, each pause a song,
In the stillness, we all belong.

So close your eyes, let slumber weave,
The magic of night, just believe.
With dreams kissed by the stars above,
Awaken in peace, embraced by love.

Wandering Through White

Wandering paths in a world so white,
Every step feels pure, feels right.
Snowflakes swirl in the gentlest dance,
Each moment invites a fleeting glance.

Trees stand tall, cloaked in white,
Guardians of the silent night.
Footfalls lead where shadows hide,
In winter's grip, there's nowhere to bide.

The air is crisp, filled with cheer,
As thoughts drift on winter's veneer.
A quiet beauty wraps the ground,
In this stillness, peace is found.

Frosted whispers kiss the air,
Nature's painting, beyond compare.
With every breath, a story told,
In the embrace of winter's cold.

So wander on with heart alight,
Through fields that stretch, pure and bright.
For in this white, we find our place,
In winter's arms, a warm embrace.

Milton Keynes UK
Ingram Content Group UK Ltd.
UKHW010228111224
452348UK00011B/586